C000272618

Edited by
ANDREW ROBERTS
NEIL JOHNSON
and **TOM MILTON**

EATING TOGETHER

66 They broke bread in their homes
and **ate together** with glad and sincere
hearts, praising God and enjoying **99**
the favour of all the people.

The Bible Reading Fellowship
15 The Chambers, Vineyard
Abingdon OX14 3FE
brf.org.uk

The Bible Reading Fellowship (BRF) is a Registered Charity (233280)

ISBN 978 0 85746 684 6
First published 2018
10 9 8 7 6 5 4 3 2 1 0
All rights reserved

Acknowledgements
Unless otherwise acknowledged, scripture quotations from The New Revised Standard
Version of the Bible, Anglicised edition, copyright © 1989, 1995 by the Division of Christian
Education of the National Council of the churches of Christ in the United States of
America. Used by permission. All rights reserved.

Scripture quotations on cover and title page, or marked NIV, are taken from The Holy
Bible, New International Version (Anglicised edition) copyright © 1979, 1984, 2011 by
Biblica. Used by permission of Hodder & Stoughton Publishers, a Hachette UK company.
All rights reserved. 'NIV' is a registered trademark of Biblica. UK trademark number
1448790.

Scripture quotations taken from the Holy Bible, New Living Translation, copyright © 1996,
2004, 2007, 2013. Used by permission of Tyndale House Publishers, Inc., Carol Stream,
Illinois 60188. All rights reserved.

Photographs on pages 11 and 43 copyright © Thinkstock; photographs on pages 4, 21, 26,
39 and 62 copyright © Tom Milton and the Birmingham Methodist Circuit; photograph on
page 41 copyright © Jane Lewis.

Every effort has been made to trace and contact copyright owners for material used in
this resource. We apologise for any inadvertent omissions or errors, and would ask those
concerned to contact us so that full acknowledgement can be made in the future.

A catalogue record for this book is available from the British Library

Printed and bound by CPI Group (UK) Ltd, Croydon CR0 4YY

CONTENTS

To order more copies of the Holy Habits resources, or to find out how to download pages for printing or projection on screen, please visit brfonline.org.uk/holy-habits.

Remember the context

This Holy Habit is set in the context of ten Holy Habits, and the ongoing life of your church and community.

> They devoted themselves to the apostles' teaching and fellowship, to the breaking of bread and the prayers. Awe came upon everyone, because many wonders and signs were being done by the apostles. All who believed were together and had all things in common; they would sell their possessions and goods and distribute the proceeds to all, as any had need. Day by day, as they spent much time together in the temple, they broke bread at home and **ate their food** with glad and generous hearts, praising God and having the goodwill of all the people. And day by day the Lord added to their number those who were being saved.
>
> ACTS 2:42–47

A prayer for the faithful practice of Holy Habits

This prayer starts with a passage from Romans 5:4–5.

> Endurance produces character, and character produces hope,
>   and hope does not disappoint us...
> Gracious and ever-loving God, we offer our lives to you.
> Help us always to be open to your Spirit in our thoughts
>   and feelings and actions.
> Support us as we seek to learn more about those habits of the Christian life
>   which, as we practise them, will form in us the character of Jesus
>   by establishing us in the way of faith, hope and love.
> Amen

INTRODUCTION

Welcome to **Eating Together**! The tradition of people **Eating Together** being a sign of God's reign or kingdom goes way back into Judaeo-Christian history. It is a picture painted by the prophets and celebrated in the psalms:

> On this mountain the Lord of hosts will make for all peoples a feast of rich food, a feast of well-matured wines, of rich food filled with marrow, of well-matured wines strained clear.
>
> ISAIAH 25:6

> You prepare a table before me in the presence of my enemies; you anoint my head with oil; my cup overflows.
>
> PSALM 23:5

Jesus was rooted in and lived this tradition. Just as he shared food with all sorts and conditions of people as a sign of the inclusivity of God's kingdom, so too did the early church. The gatherings to **Eat Together** were earthly representations of the heavenly banquet imagery that had been reinforced by Jesus through his teaching as well as his actions. Following in the footsteps of Jesus, the table fellowship of the early Christians was warm and accepting. They refused to discriminate against the marginalised. All were welcome to partake of this basic human and yet deeply sacred activity.

The joy of **Eating Together**, the value of table fellowship for deepening relationships, the missional fruitfulness of shared meals and the opportunities for sharing faith, biblical study, prayer and worship around the meal table have all been rediscovered many times by both new and ancient forms of church. Holy Habits provides another opportunity to explore and live this godly practice.

Reflections

At first glance, the Holy Habit of **Eating Together** seems like an easy one. Many of us enjoy eating together with family and friends and eating together is often a regular feature of church life. But this Holy Habit invites us to do more than simply consume food. It invites us to explore how we **Eat Together** and with whom.

Jesus was often criticised for who he chose to eat with. The feeding of the 5,000 in John's Gospel (John 6:1–14) starts with a boy and his little picnic of five loaves and two fishes and ends with a meal for 5,000 people. This story demonstrate the generous love of God and invite us to share what we have with **Gladness and Generosity**.

- It's easy to eat with friends and family, but what about those we don't know? Do we need to explore **Eating Together** with them?
- How can we share food with those who use our premises and the wider community?
- How often do we eat with our neighbours or those in our street?
- And what about the person for whom eating with others is difficult?
- How can we be inclusive of those who are unable to eat freely for health reasons, those with diabetes, allergies or food intolerances, those with eating disorders?
- Can we share those aspects of **Eating Together** which do not involve food?

As you consider the importance of **Eating Together**, could you be people who EAT with **E**quality, **A**ffirmation and **T**ogetherness in true **Fellowship** with all?

> Please remember to consider the needs of those with special dietary requirements including diabetes, food allergies or intolerances, eating disorders or other restrictions around food and drink.

  Resources particularly suitable for children and families

☺ Resources particularly suitable for young people

CH4 Church Hymnary 4 (also known as Hymns of Glory Songs of Praise)
RS Rejoice and Sing
SoF Songs of Fellowship 6
StF Singing the Faith

UNDERSTANDING THE HABIT

WORSHIP RESOURCES

Below are some thoughts and ideas on how you might incorporate this Holy Habit into worship.

Biblical material

Old Testament passages:

- Genesis 18:1–10   Abraham entertaining angels
- 1 Kings 17:8–15   Elijah and the widow
- Isaiah 25:6–9   A heavenly banquet

Gospel passages:

- Luke 10:38–42   Mary and Martha
- Luke 14:15–24   The great feast
- Luke 15:11–32   The great feast part 2 (or the prodigal son)
- Luke 19:1–9   Zacchaeus
- John 2:1–11   Wedding at Cana
- John 6:1–15   Feeding of the 5,000
- John 21:1–14   Breakfast on the beach

Other New Testament passages:

- Acts 10:9–28   Peter's objection to table fellowship with Gentiles demolished
- 1 Corinthians 11:17–22   Rich and poor instructed to share together fully

Suggested hymns and songs

- Come, and let us sweetly join (StF 646)
- Come as you are (SoF 2754) ☺
- Come, sinners, to the gospel feast (StF 401)
- God bless to us our bread (CH4 763)
- God's table (*Iona Community Wild Goose Songs*, Volume 1, p. 92)
- Have you heard God's voice (StF 662)
- Help us accept each other (RS 646)
- I, the Lord of sea and sky (CH4 251, StF 663)
- Jesus Christ is waiting (CH4 360, StF 251)
- Let us build a house (all are welcome) (CH4 198, StF 409)
- Living God your joyful Spirit (RS 530)
- Summoned by the God who made us (StF 689)
- The church is like a table (RS 480)
- The kingdom of God (RS 200, StF 255)
- The trumpets sound (StF 35)
- We are your people (RS 483)

Introduction to the theme 👪

You will need:

- Two small tables (or one larger one) and two chairs
- Two glasses, one with orange juice and the other with a mix of non-alcoholic ginger beer and water (or something similar – the aim is to make a drink that looks unappetising)
- A nice inviting piece of food such as sweets or a small piece of cake, and a less inviting piece of food such as a partially torn lettuce leaf.

Invite two volunteers forward for a quiz. The quiz can be on the subject of a famous Bible reading, or you could have one of the lessons for the day read first and that can form the subject of the quiz.

You will need around four to six questions (two or three for each contestant). It is important that the contestants get the answer correct. Make the questions relatively easy and help the contestants to 'ask the audience' so that they can be confident of the right answer. Reward each right answer with a prize.

For the first round give:
- Beautiful freshly squeezed orange juice to contestant one
- Ginger beer mixed with water to contestant two.

For the second round give:
- The finest chocolate cake (or some other tasty treat) to contestant one
- The lettuce leaf to contestant two.

The aim is to show blatant favouritism. Make a show of the loveliness of the prizes for contestant one, pretend to be uninterested in contestant two. Make it as much fun as you can. Finally, give the contestants a round of applause and send them back to their seats.

Read 1 Corinthians 11:17–22.

Explain that the kind of favouritism seen in the quiz has actually been seen in churches. Paul was cross with the church at Corinth because of their eating practices, which seemed to reward some more than others! Our **Eating Together** should be a powerful sign and demonstration of our togetherness – not our differences (11:33).

Thoughts for sermon preparation

Luke 15:11–32

This is a parable about **Eating Together** in a great feast. It is, of course, often described as the parable of the 'prodigal son', who, as it were, captures the headlines. But it is also about another son, a father and, above all, a shared feast.

In the time of Jesus, when a father who had two sons died, the elder would get two-thirds of his property and the younger one-third. A father could, however, pass over parts of his property to his sons in his lifetime. In that case, the sons were meant to use the property for the benefit of the whole family, and the father was still supposed to benefit from the income or other produce from the property. This, though, could not be guaranteed, and Ecclesiasticus 33:19–23, in the Apocrypha, points to the risks.

In this particular story, in response to a request from the younger son, the father divides the property between both sons (v. 12). The younger son proceeds to ignore any further responsibility that he might have to his family. He capitalises his assets and goes far away, where he squanders his money. Note that we are not told exactly how; we are left to fantasise about it, just as the elder brother does later in the story. But the important point is the squandering of the wealth.

Disaster then strikes. A famine comes, and the younger son is not able to look after himself. He ends up not just having to work for a Gentile but feeding his pigs, which for Jews was a forbidden occupation with unclean animals. Just as he had ceased to care for his own family, now nobody looks after him (v. 16). All he has to eat is the food of the pigs, on his own. He has hit rock bottom.

He comes to his senses and returns to face his father. His father does not wait for him to grovel but rushes out to welcome him. The son has rehearsed what he will say. He gets as far as saying that he does not deserve to be counted as a son, but the father stops him before he can ask to be treated as a servant. His father reinstates him as a son with a new robe, a ring and sandals, and orders a feast to celebrate.

The feast is generous and extravagant. The calf is one that has been kept and fattened for a very special occasion (v. 23). The celebration is joyful and fun, and accompanied with music and dancing (v. 25). This is not one of those religious occasions where the only enjoyment to be had is in not showing to anyone that you are enjoying it!

But the story does not end there. There is another son. He turns out to be resentful and jealous. He has not capitalised his share of the property, but stayed at home working for the family's benefit. What happens, though, shows that, despite outward appearances, he too has become distanced from his father. He does not speak respectfully to his father. He criticises him, and casts aspersions on his brother to make him appear in a worse light (there is no evidence in the story that the way the younger brother has squandered his money is by spending it on prostitutes!). He may be angry that he will lose out by the reinstatement of his younger brother. He refuses to join the celebration. But the father goes out to meet him (v. 28), like he goes out to meet the younger son (v. 20). The father seeks out and rejoices first, and looks to sort other things out afterwards. The younger son repents by reconnecting with his father and changing his attitudes and behaviour. Will the elder? Would you?

The point is that this meal is for them all, deserved or not, with or without repentance. It is a gift of love that creates love. It is like God's overflowing love for us, which makes us overflow with love for others. **Eating Together** is a response to that love.

Do we offer opportunities to **Eat Together** to others in our individual lives and our church life? Who are we like in Jesus' story: the father, the younger son or the elder one?

Prayers

A short prayer which could be used regularly to focus on this Holy Habit

Most loving God,
You are the source of all life,
the Sustainer and Renewer of each one of us.
We offer our thanks to you for the provision of food to nourish our bodies,
and for how the opportunity to eat together nourishes our souls.
Throughout the history of your people,
table fellowship has challenged prejudices,
broken down barriers,
and created communities.
At the heart of Jesus' ministry was the sharing of food
as a taste of your New World.
In the name of Jesus, let us eat together,
share our common resources,
and struggle for a just distribution of all the good gifts around us.
Amen

A prayer of praise and thanksgiving

Creator God,
We thank you for your creative energy which began life on our planet,
and for your sustaining power upholding this awesome creation today.
We are amazed and humbled by the vast variety of your creation.
In particular today, we praise you for all the different things we have to eat –
different flavours, different textures, different tastes.
We offer you our grateful thanks for foods that give strength to our bodies.

Saviour God,
We praise you for your constant love and forgiveness
surrounding us every day.
We express our thanks for your promise of abundant and eternal life.
As we think of the cross and the empty tomb,
we thank you that you offer us food for our souls as well as our bodies.
We praise you for the way our souls have been nourished and nurtured.

We ask your blessing on our continuing spiritual growth
as congregations and individuals.

Spirit of God,
You draw us together as we pray.
You draw us together as we worship.
You draw us together as we eat together.

As we share together in worship, in food and in fellowship,
unite us as your people.
Make us a people where all are invited,
all are welcome,
all are equal around your table.
So may we look forward to sharing your heavenly banquet
where strangers become friends.
Amen

A prayer of confession

Read aloud John 21:15–17.

Like Peter by the lake, Lord,
we don't even know the ways in which we need your forgiveness.
The smell of food by the lake reminds us of more innocent days
and timeless lapping of the waters draws us close.
We want to sit and eat with you, to be held spellbound in your company,
but first we must make amends.

You told us over and over and over that
when we fed those who were hungry,
we were feeding you;
that when we did your work,
we would find ourselves in the people who needed us.
Yet sometimes we have not shared,
sometimes we have forgotten you
and sometimes we have rejected the free gift of love.

For the times when we denied you,
hid from you and walked away,
for the people we have wronged and the actions we regret,
we humbly beg your forgiveness.

For all those we did not feed, and for the mercy we rejected,
we ask your forgiveness.
For all the things we did not do,
refused to do, felt unworthy to do,
we ask your forgiveness.

(*Silence*)

God grant us your understanding
and, like Peter, show us how we might serve.
You have told us again and again and again that the waters of life
will wash us clean,
that our place at the table will always be free
and that in you there is always hope.
Take away the burdens we carry and bring us close.
Let us eat together again.

We thank you and pray all these prayers in the name of your son Jesus Christ.
Amen

A prayer of intercession

You may choose to use the response 'Lord, hear our prayer' or not.

We pray together as we eat together.
We come before you, Lord, in all our hunger for a better world
and ask that you hear our prayers.

For starters,
we remember and bring before you a thousand small prayers of need –
to help and walk alongside those who feed us, love us and bring us hope.
We think of those who serve in so many roles,
and particularly those who work in the food industry.
The multiplicity and diversity of cultures and cuisines
are brought to us by so many often-forgotten people.
From supermarket to restaurant and beyond,
we ask that you protect our low-paid and our under-represented.

Lord, hear our prayer

We think of those who offer themselves in helping others:
the food bank workers, home helpers and carers,
givers of gifts and donators of tins, charity workers and encouragers,
bakers of cakes and washers of plates.

Lord, hear our prayer

Our main course prayers
are for those who suffer on a worldwide scale:
Lord, we ask that you bring hope to areas of conflict and peace
to the hearts and souls of those who have not enough.

Lord, hear our prayer

We pray for just desserts:
for the eradication of hunger and causes of poverty.
We pray for the needs of a growing population
and about the disparity of opportunity.
Help us to play our part in bringing justice and redressing the balance.
Help us to model your sharing of resources:
that we might have what we need,
but also that we might be part of your overflowing cup of life.

Lord, hear our prayer

We pray for our friends and family,
those who are closest to us, that we might all know the joy of company,
freedom from worry, and the abundance of your kingdom.

In the quiet, we bring before you
all those we have particular concerns for at this time.

(*Silence*)

Lord, hear our prayer

We bring our prayers in the name of God the great provider,
in the name of Christ who ate with us
and in the name of the Holy Spirit who sustains us.

Amen

A prayer of sending out and blessing

A prayer which uses Jude 24–25 (NLT) as its final paragraph.

Generous God, in all that we do this week
Help us to taste and see that you are good.

Welcoming God, in all that we are this week
Help us to be open and hospitable to those that we meet.

Encouraging God, in all that we think this week
Help us to know that anything is possible with you.

Now all glory to God,
who is able to keep you from falling away
and will bring you with great joy into his glorious presence
without a single fault.
All glory to him who alone is God,
our Saviour through Jesus Christ our Lord.
All glory, majesty, power, and authority are his before all time,
and in the present, and beyond all time!
Amen

A simple grace for a frugal lunch

Dear God, we have been joined together
by our faith,
by our concern for the world,
by this simple meal.

Though our bodies may be satisfied,
keep us hungry for justice,
working together to make your kingdom known.
Amen

Café church/café worship

Café church is one of the more popular forms of fresh expression of church that has been developing in recent years. Alongside café churches (meeting in cafés and coffee shops), café worship has been developed by many churches on their premises as part of the range of **Worship** opportunities they offer. Both have **Eating Together** at the centre of what they do.

The cafechurch network – founded and led by the delightfully named Cid Latty – is a prime example of café church formed primarily for those who are not yet disciples of Jesus. In an interview with Fresh Expressions, Cid explained:

> cafechurch is all about creating a context for people who do not go to 'church', but are interested in God. It is about providing a comfortable setting for people to consider issues from a faith perspective. It is also a way to develop a community that people are happy to be a part of. All this is based on good incarnational theology.
> community.sharetheguide.org/stories/cafechurchnetwork

On the cafechurch website Cid goes on to explain:

> cafechurch is coffee with a conscience. It's the fresh expression of community in high street coffee stores (primarily Costa Coffee stores), dealing with issues from a faith perspective.
>
> At cafechurch, you'll tackle issues such as fair trade, the environment, stress, adoption, parenting, debt and divorce, together with quizzes, interviews, round table discussions, live music with great coffee and great chat!'
> www.cafechurch.net/index.php?module=pagemaster&PAGE_user_op=view_page&PAGE_id=10

In this short resume, we see a number of Holy Habits in operation: **Eating Together**, **Fellowship** and **Serving**, to name just three. Other habits may need to be introduced carefully in a context primarily developed for 'those who don't do church'.

The practice of these habits is likely to be part of café worship that is part of the life of an existing church. In forming café worship it is vital to take to time to craft an act of worship that is both accessible to those who are not yet disciples of Jesus (if the intent is at least in part evangelistic) and fits the conversational, relaxed context. Don't just move the normal worship practice form one space to another! Café worship can be particularly helpful way of to explore ways of **Breaking Bread** other than Holy Communion.

Different ways of praying

A prayer of commitment: water into wine

Jesus transformed water into wine at the wedding in Cana of Galilee (John 2). Jesus seeks to transform us too.

Drop some red fruit squash concentrate (preferably double strength) into a glass of water. See how it begins to spread. How has the Spirit of Jesus begun to spread his influence into different areas of your life?

Stir the water with a teaspoon until all the water in the glass is coloured. How do you need the gift of God's grace to be stirred up within your life?

Bible verse cookies

Make fortune cookies (there are recipes on the internet) and place Bible verses inside.

Exchange the cookies, or make them for your church. Take them to the housebound (and **Eat Together**). Could you give them out in your community – to passers-by outside your church doors, in the local shopping centre, at transport hubs, in a local market? Make sure you get appropriate permission from the location.

You can print out the full verses or just include the Bible reference depending on your audience.

(This could also be part of an **Eating Together** activity when exploring the **Biblical Teaching** Holy Habit).

Prayer plate

When sharing food with large groups of people, time can be an issue. It may then be difficult to include prayers or other religious content. The meal may also include a very wide range of ages, experience and levels of understanding. Prayers, greetings or ideas might be written or printed on paper plates. (Professional printers offer a service putting messages on party plates, cups and beer mats.) These prayers were written during a meal.

Written circularly around a plate:

Break now the circle of injustice that allows one person to have so much and another so little. Break now the circle of debt and tax evasion that leaves our governments powerless to improve services. Break now the circle of conflict that forces authorities to spend money on arms instead of food. Break now the circle of fear and despair in developing countries. Help us to seek the answers to world hunger. Amen.

A grace:

Lord, grace this table with your presence.
Help us to feel you close, to know the love of Jesus
Through the closeness of our friends, the sharing in this banquet
and the fellowship therein.
We thank you for your glory and forgiveness of our sins.
Amen

A prayer of thanksgiving: taste and see

Take a grape or a piece of chocolate. As you enjoy the taste, give thanks to God for all that is good in your life and know that God is good.

Pizza prayers

Everyone contributes a slice!

Cut a circle of paper into segments and give one to everyone present. On one side draw (or write) your favourite pizza topping, and on the other write one short line of a grace or draw something for which you are thankful.

The segments are returned to the table centre, topping side up, to form everyone's favourite pizza. Before the meal begins each person takes a slice at random and they are read out in turn.

Six slices is generally enough for one pizza prayer – for larger group sizes, make several pizzas and pray grace in small groups.

Or you could adapt this idea and make real pizza...

GROUP MATERIAL AND ACTIVITIES

Some of these small group materials are traditional Bible studies, some are more diverse session plans and others are short activities, reflections and discussions. Please choose materials appropriate to whatever group you are working with.

Breakfast on the beach

John 21:1–14

Whenever we gather, it is good to share food and drink. This study in particular should involve the sharing of food – as simple as coffee, tea and biscuits, or bring-and-share finger food. Please note this will need planning in advance and, again, be mindful of allergens and other food-related issues.

1 Welcome

Welcome everyone and invite them to introduce themselves by saying their name and finishing the following sentence, 'One of the best meals I've ever had was…'

2 Prayer

Thank God:

- for our ability and freedom to meet
- for God's promise to be with us as we meet
- for the way God provides for our needs and feeds us – physically, mentally, spiritually, emotionally. May we be open to each other, God's word and the Holy Spirit as we meet.

3 Introducing the Bible reading

John 21:1–14 – breakfast on the beach

- Introduce the passage. What type of material are we dealing with – for example, letter, history, gospel, law, prophecy?

- What is the context of the passage – what comes before and after? Who's speaking? Who to? Why?

4 Bible study

- Read the passage from one translation while others follow in their translations.
- Read the same passage from another, quite different, translation.
- Compare and contrast the language and emphasis of the different versions.
- Are there any links, connections or echoes of other Bible stories?

5 Small group work

- If you are able to, divide the study group into three or more smaller groups (three to five people). Each group takes the role of one of the characters in the story (Jesus, Peter, other disciples). In the small groups, discuss the story from your character's perspective, and be prepared to retell your story from a first-person perspective (I, we, etc.). Feel free to fill in aspects of the story (pay attention to the context, the feelings of the characters). Come back together, and share your character's story from the first-person perspective – Jesus, Peter, other disciples).
- If the group is small and it is not possible to divide into smaller groups, stay in the one group and as a group take the role of one of the characters in the story. Discuss it from the first-person perspective for five to ten minutes, then move on to the other two characters and do the same.

6 Questions

Look at some or all of these questions, or you may use your own.

- Compare and contrast the following: a snack, a meal, a banquet, a feast.
- In the story of the breakfast on the beach, who is the host?
- Is the breakfast a meal, a banquet or a feast?
- In 2003, the Methodist Church brought out a publication about Communion entitled 'His presence makes the feast'. From the title, what do we think it is trying to say? If there are members of the group who have read it, they might like to share their thoughts. Some people might like to read it.
- Read Psalm 36:5–9. What does this say about God? Is this a different message from the breakfast on the beach?

7 **Plan a meal**

Relationships change when you've had a meal with someone.

- Think of someone you would like to have a meal with, for no other reason than to sit and eat with them (a neighbour, a friend, a family member, a church member). Pray for them.
- Think of a group of people for whom the church could host a meal. Who are they? Where are they? Where would you hold the meal? When would you hold the meal? How might this become a regular (habitual) event, perhaps quarterly or monthly or around the time of festivals such as Pentecost, Harvest and Christmas? Pray:
  - for them
  - that God will go ahead of you, and prepare their hearts and minds
  - for wisdom and discernment in handling this meal
- Might gathering around a meal be the starting point for a new small group, cell group or new monastic community?

8 **Share a grace and Eat Together.**

The great banquet 👪 Luke 14:15–24

Prayer

Ask someone from the group to say grace. They could use one of the following:

- Bless this food to our bodies and us to your service. In Jesus' name we pray. Amen.
- For what we are about to receive, may the Lord make us truly thankful.
- Heavenly Pa, ta.

Share a small snack such as grapes, cheese and biscuits or chocolate sweets.

Discussion

This can be started while the snack is being eaten.

- Who likes food?
- What is your favourite meal?
- Do you like having others eat with you?

- If you were having a special meal, who would you like to invite? How many guests would you invite to your special meal?
- If you could invite anyone famous to a dinner party or meal, who would you like to invite?
- Are there any people you wouldn't like to come?

Bible study

Read Luke 14:15–24.

- Who is the host in the story and why was he throwing a party?
- What was it that the host didn't like and what was his response?
- What does this tell us about the host?

(Try to ensure that people see that the host in the story doesn't want to eat on his own – he is desperate that his banquet should be full and this is almost certainly the cause of his frustration. He wants as many guests to come and share in the banquet as he can possibly fit in.)

Activities

Grace
Discuss: Why do you think people say grace at the beginning of a meal?

Write some different graces, thinking carefully about what you want to say in them.

Challenge people to say grace before each meal for a week. They could use the graces that they have written. The next time you meet, ask them what it felt like to say grace before every meal. Did it change anything or make them feel differently about the meal?

Homeless feast
The Fowlers (from Atlanta, USA) had paid in advance for their daughter's wedding, only to find that the couple decided not to marry! They decided to keep the booking but give the four-course meal to the homeless. This story can be found on a number of news websites, for example: **www.nydailynews.com/news/national/homeless-enjoy-woman-canceled-wedding-article-1.1464704.**

Take some time to discuss what people think about this story and whether the couple did the right thing.

Wall poster

Make a wall poster entitled 'The Great Banquet'.

People can all contribute to the poster by drawing and colouring a picture of their favourite food. Hopefully, all the pictures together will give the effect of a banquet ready to be shared!

You could include the quote, 'Go out to the roads and country lanes and compel them to come in, so that my house will be full' (Luke 14:23, NIV).

This activity could be very time-consuming. Depending on how many people you think you will have, you may need to have the letters for the heading ('The Great Banquet') and the quote from verse 23 printed and ready to be coloured in.

Party planning

If you have extra time, you could invite people to plan their next party. What food? What music? What games? Who should they invite?

Final prayers

Ensure everybody has some time to do this. These prayers take the form of RSVP cards:

Lord God, thank you for inviting us to your banquet.
I would like to come and be part of it because…

Story sack 👪 John 6:1–15

Retell the story of the five loaves and two fishes (based on John 6:1–15) in your own words, or using one of the many scripts available, involving the group in the telling of the story. You could prepare a sack containing two cardboard fish, five small bread rolls, a basket, a cloth and a cloak, and use these props during the story.

For younger children, you could ask them to join in actions for the story (e.g. walking slowly and tiredly following Jesus as he teaches, listening, being hungry, eating the bread and fish).

For others, you may want to ask them to dramatise the story themselves.

Make sure you finish by sharing the bread!

Chocolate trade game ☺

This game, from Christian Aid, traces the journey of the cocoa bean from tree to chocolate bar and explores the difficulties workers in the chocolate trade face.

Visit **learn.christianaid.org.uk/YouthLeaderResources/choc_trade.aspx** or search **www.christianaid.org.uk/learn** for 'Chocolate Trade Game'.

Handa's Surprise 👪

This is based on the beautiful book *Handa's Surprise* by Eileen Browne (Scholastic/ Walker Books, 2006), which is particularly suitable for younger children.

Handa takes a carefully chosen basket of fruit to her friend but, on the way, different animals take a piece of fruit from the basket, which is balanced on her head. She ends up with a basket of a different fruit and her friend is delighted.

- Try acting out this story with real fruit.
- Use the fruit to make a fruit salad and eat it together.
- How does each piece of fruit add to the fruit salad?
- How did each person add to the fruit salad?

The Soup Stone 👪

Share the story of the Soup Stone as a discussion starter:

A stranger arrived at a villager's door asking for something to eat. The villager explained that she had nothing to spare. The stranger smiled and told the villager not to worry; with the soup stone in his bag, he would be able to cook up some delicious soup if the villager would provide him with a pot of water.

The villager was curious, so she dragged out her biggest pot and filled it with water. As the stranger began preparations for the soup by dropping his soup stone in the pot, a crowd of interested neighbours began to gather.

As the water began to boil, the stranger tasted the soup. He pronounced it was delicious but just needed some potatoes. A neighbour dashed off to her kitchen and returned with a large quantity of sliced potatoes.

After the potatoes had been added, the stranger tasted the soup again and commented that it would become a lovely stew if they had a little meat. At these words, another neighbour disappeared to her kitchen, returning with some tender meat.

With one final taste, the stranger declared that the finishing touch would be some seasoning. As if by magic, a villager popped up with salt and pepper.

Giving the soup one last stir, the stranger announced, 'Bowls for everyone!' Villagers ran into their kitchens for bowls and some also returned with bread and fruit. The stranger ladled out large helpings of the tasty soup for everyone.

Everyone laughed and talked as they shared their first common meal. During the excited chatter, the stranger silently slipped away. However, he left behind the miraculous soup stone with which the villagers could make the loveliest soup in the world any time they wanted.

FORMING THE HABIT

The ideas presented in this section are offered to help you establish or practise **Eating Together** as a regular habit personally, as a church and in engagement with your local community and the wider world. You may want to consider using the ideas in more than one of these contexts.

In developing **Eating Together** as a regular habit, you may find some of the material in the 'Understanding the habit' section helpful too.

STORIES TO SHOW THE HABIT FORMING

How could you use these formative and transformative stories to inspire others? What stories of your own could you share?

Eating Together is transformational missional activity. It is also a great way to build relationships within and across cultures. In his book *Holy Habits* (Malcolm Down Publishing, 2016), Andrew Roberts shares these stories:

> One of the most memorable meals I have shared was with some homeless men on Princes Street in Edinburgh. I was working in the city a few days before Christmas and went to visit the German market on the garden side of the street. The market was alive with light, music, laughter and all sorts of treats to buy and eat. On the other side of the street, the homeless men were beginning to bed in for the night, in the cold, in the shop entrances. I went back to the market and got some food and took it across to share with some of them. It was a holy moment. Their gratitude and smiles were as bright as the lights across the road. As we parted, the mutual expressions of 'God bless' were as alive as if the one born outside in a stable whose birth we were celebrating had been physically there pronouncing God's blessing himself.

> When I was working in the Caribbean, there was a bank holiday and so I went for a walk. I came to a park where families and church groups were playing cricket and enjoying picnics. I was very obviously not a local (the pale complexion was a giveaway), but a total stranger, thousands of miles from home. 'Come over and join us' came the cry from one group who warmly welcomed me, engaging me in conversation and determinedly plying me with all manner of tasty Bajan treats – the matriarchs in the group seemingly keen to put some fat on my less than muscle-bound physique. I had a glorious time. A little bit of heaven in paradise. And I learned a lot about the value of hospitality, the welcoming of strangers and the sharing of food in building relationships and revealing the kingdom.

From the Moravians to the Methodists and in other Christian traditions too, the Love Feast has proved to be a gracious and energising gift in **Eating Together**. Rachel Parkinson (Chair of the Wolverhampton and Shrewsbury District) tells how this practice has impacted her and how it is a practice whose time may have come again for the formation and nurture of followers of Jesus.

The Love Feast gift was given to me when I helped to lead a Love Feast at the Methodist Conference in Southport in 2015. As I watched small groups tucking into fruited tear'n'share bread baked for us by the 'Somewhere Else' Bread Church in Liverpool, and heard people joyfully and comfortably witnessing to the activity of the Holy Spirit in their lives, I knew that the Love Feast was not simply to be dusted off once in a blue moon. At a time when we recognise how important it is to develop confidence in talking about God in our everyday lives, here was a simple form of worship which encourages us to do exactly that. Since then, I have led Love Feasts in a variety of contexts, from tiny congregations to a District Synod.

The Love Feast (or Agape) goes back to a time in the early church when it is believed that the sacramental sharing of bread and wine was often part of a larger meal shared by Christian communities. Before long, the 'Eucharist' and 'Agape' became separate celebrations, following which the latter dropped out of use. Upon its revival in the 18th century, John Wesley encountered it through the Moravians. Quickly spotting its potential, Wesley introduced it to Methodist practice, where it became a powerful means of revival in many places. As people shared food and drink, they sang joyfully, prayed with passion and found a wonderful freedom to testify to the work of God. However, as the 19th century progressed and church life became both more ordered and less spontaneous, the Love Feast once again dropped out of fashion.

I believe it's time for another revival. We need not be bound by past convention. While taking care not to confuse a Love Feast with the Lord's Supper, we need only to heed what John Wesley told the congregation gathered at Birstall in 1761: 'The very design of a Love Feast is free and familiar conversation in which every man, yea and woman, has liberty to speak whatever may be to the glory of God.'

A liturgy for a Love Feast service can be found in the **Gladness and Generosity** Holy Habit booklet.

PRACTICES TO HELP FORM THE HABIT

Here are some suggestions for how **Eating Together** can be part of a rhythm or rule of life in our personal discipleship and in and through the **Fellowship** of our churches.

Eating Together can be a particularly effective way of helping small groups form and opening up conversations.

Some fresh expressions of church have begun with friends meeting around a table and exploring the call and claims of Jesus. Might you form something new in this way?

For established groups, consider how a meal or series of meals might be an aid to the renewal of the group. Alternatively, challenge yourselves to offer, or partner with others in offering, meals to those on the margins of society for whom **Eating Together** may be just a dream.

As a church, could you regularly address some or all of the 'Questions to consider as a church' (p. 44) in your church's life and meetings?

Often (daily or weekly)

Journalling

Journalling is regularly reflecting on your experiences, thoughts and encounters with God and keeping a note of your reflections. See the Holy Habits Introductory Guide for more information.

As you try different ways of **Eating Together**, note in your journal what you did and how you felt, and anything in particular that was a positive experience. Were there any ways of **Eating Together** that you particularly struggled with? Did some ways feel more comfortable than others? Has it changed your relationships with people? Reflect as you look back in your journal – how was God acting in your life through **Eating Together** with others?

Eat together 👪 ☺

If you live with others, take time each day to eat or drink together and share your stories and your concerns for others. If you live alone, how could you make **Eating Together** with others part of your routine? Are there creative ways you can share food or drink with others – through invitation or using video calling (e.g. Skype)?

Consider whether there are people in your community who do not have opportunity to eat or drink with others on a regular basis. How could you create those opportunities?

Plan a programme of opportunities to **Eat Together** as a church and with the community. For example:

- Have a 'Bring and Share' evening where people bring a dish and the recipe. You could go on to create a recipe book (taking care not to infringe any copyrights).
- Arrange a whole church meal, BBQ, picnic or similar, remembering to include those who might get overlooked or forgotten. Be inspired by the parable of the great feast (Luke 14:15–24) to extend this to a community meal for those who are on the fringes of church life or society, those who live next door to our buildings or people who have a common bond (single parents and children or lonely older people, for example).
- Hold a cooking competition like the *Great British Bake Off* or *Ready Steady Cook*. Mix up teams of adults and younger people.
- Begin at someone's house for a starter, move on to somebody else's house for main course and somewhere else again for pudding.

- Invite your friends or community to a posh banquet. You could have a chocolate fountain, or cocktails/mocktails.
- Hold a teddy bears' picnic at which you share the feeding of the 5,000 story.
- Have a beach-themed party with ice creams and the opportunity to share any of the stories of Jesus on the beach with his disciples.

Alternatively, you might like to take up a challenge and commit to **Eating Together** as a small group, youth group or congregation once a week for half a term. At the end of the half term, share reflections on what it was like to **Eat Together** and whether anything changed or felt different after six weeks of doing this.

Say grace

Consider saying a grace before meals – every meal, once a day or once a week, depending on the rhythm of your life.

For example:

> For food to enjoy,
> For friends and family to share it with,
> For the commitment to end poverty and hunger,
> We thank you, God of all.
> Amen

If you already do say grace, try increasing how often, or explore different ways of saying grace – for example, singing grace or using a 'grace dice'.

Could you encourage church members to find a grace and share it each week before refreshments at the end of the service, or even before Communion? The congregation could be invited to learn the grace and use it during the week in their homes.

There are plenty of books of graces available which you could use at home or in your church **Worship** or **Fellowship**. For example:

Dilly Baker, *A Place at the Table: Liturgies and resources for Christ-centred hospitality* (Canterbury Press, 2008).
Neil Paynter, *Blessed Be Our Table: Graces for mealtimes and reflections on food* (Wild Goose Publications, 2003) 🖐

Share food

Offer refreshments and hospitality to any groups that share your premises.

Consider providing a regular meal for those in particular need in your community as an act of love and service.

Seasonal cooking

As part of a rhythm of life for yourself or your church, try cooking with seasonal food where possible.

Check out the BBC Good Food 'Seasonality table' (**www.bbcgoodfood.com/ seasonal-calendar/all**) where you can see what is in season and then plan your shopping accordingly. A local greengrocer, if you have one, may also be able to advise on seasonal fruit and vegetables.

Sometimes (weekly or monthly)

Eat in a different way

Sample the food of another culture and, in so doing, learn about and celebrate that culture. You could make a point of eating with someone who would otherwise eat on their own (the shy person in the office or at school, or the housebound neighbour).

Don't eat!

Fast or have only a very simple meal. Use the time saved to pray for those who regularly go hungry. Gift the money saved to charities working to provide sustainable food for those in poverty. Consider volunteering for such charities. Fasting can also be an act of solidarity with those who have little or no food. (If you do consider fasting, make sure that it is medically safe to do so.)

Consider how you may be able to give prayer and practical support to those in other countries for whom daily bread is a dream.

Messy Church ††††

Messy Church (**www.messychurch.org.uk**) has a number of ideas for building **Eating Together** into the life of your church and family, and is suited to those of all ages.

Food club

Setting up a food club is a simple idea for building relationships by regularly **Eating Together** in the workplace. Search the Evangelism Ideas website for this and a number of other food-related items, or try **www.evangelismideas.org/idea. aspx?id=141**.

Many churches run a luncheon club, providing a monthly meal for older people in particular. This is often followed by a talk or a short service – a great opportunity to combine several Holy Habits.

At the other end of the age spectrum, churches with (or seeking to attract) students have realised the value of **Eating Together**, attracting them with cooked breakfasts, pizza and other tempting fare. How might food provide an opportunity for younger people to gather to share **Fellowship** and explore faith?

Occasionally (quarterly, annually)

Celebrate the seasons

Celebrate the major Christian feasts such as Christmas, Easter and Harvest with a meal. Invite others to share in the celebration with you. Christmas in particular can be a time to welcome those who live and eat alone.

In partnership with other faith communities, could you meet together for the great feast days of various faiths and let the common need to eat be an entrée to exploring each other's traditions and beliefs?

Feed your community

For those who depend upon free school meals, school holidays can be difficult. Some churches offer a free meal service during the holidays – might you join them in offering this provision, even for one day per holiday? One such network is MakeLunch (**www.makelunch.org.uk**).

From new parents to those just out of hospital, the provision of hot meals can be almost literally a life-saver. Could your church get into the habit of providing meals to such people? It is a very gentle way of being evangelistic – being good news.

'Eat out'

Barbecues are a fantastic opportunity to meet and **Eat Together**. Encourage church members to meet their neighbours in this way. If you live near the sea, why not have a church barbecue on the beach, maybe with some simple **Worship**?

For the more adventurous, team up with the Scouts or Guides or other such groups and do some survival-skills cooking and eating at a suitable site.

Cook together

Despite seemingly endless reminders about the need to eat healthily, many still struggle to do so. Why not host or run a cookery club or course, to teach healthy cooking and eating skills? Some fresh expressions of church have formed around the practice of cooking and eating. Take a look at the story of Cook@Chapel for one good example (**community.sharetheguide.org/stories/cookatchapel**).

From the *Great British Bake Off* to *Saturday Kitchen*, cookery programmes and competitions are hugely popular. Why not host a baking or cooking competition for your local community? This could be a great way of building relationships. And if you don't have enough cooking equipment, why not ask your local secondary school if you could use their facilities for an evening? You could sweeten the ask by offering to donate proceeds from the evening to the school.

QUESTIONS TO CONSIDER AS A CHURCH

These questions will help your church to consider how it can review the place of **Eating Together** in all of its life together. They are intended to be asked regularly rather than considered once and then forgotten. You will need to determine where in your church the responsibility for each question lies – with the whole church in a general meeting, or with the church leadership, a relevant committee or another grouping. Feel free to add more of your own.

- Consider the ways in which Jesus ate with people. How does this challenge your church about the ways you do or don't share food and drink together?
- How do you show welcome with food within and around the time of **Worship**?
- Could some services be formed in a café worship style? Visit **www.cafechurch.net** or **community.sharetheguide.org/guide/examples/cafe** to explore this further.
- How can you welcome those who share your premises by sharing food with them?
- How can **Eating Together** be part of your business meetings?

- Hatches, matches and dispatches: is your church able to offer care through catering to families celebrating these milestones (births/baptism, weddings and funerals)?
- Alongside a plan for **Worship** services, can you form a plan for **Eating Together** with others, and in so doing practise and deepen several of the other habits (e.g. **Fellowship**, **Gladness and Generosity** and **Serving**)?
- How do you understand God to be present in your **Eating Together**?

CONNECTING THE HABITS

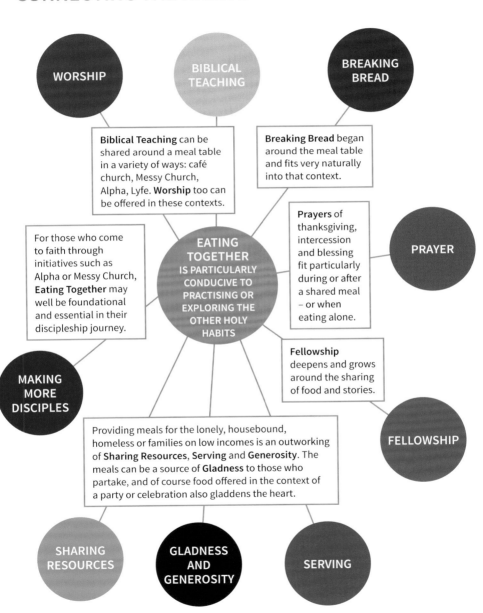

WORSHIP

BIBLICAL TEACHING

BREAKING BREAD

Biblical Teaching can be shared around a meal table in a variety of ways: café church, Messy Church, Alpha, Lyfe. **Worship** too can be offered in these contexts.

Breaking Bread began around the meal table and fits very naturally into that context.

Prayers of thanksgiving, intercession and blessing fit particularly during or after a shared meal – or when eating alone.

PRAYER

For those who come to faith through initiatives such as Alpha or Messy Church, **Eating Together** may well be foundational and essential in their discipleship journey.

EATING TOGETHER IS PARTICULARLY CONDUCIVE TO PRACTISING OR EXPLORING THE OTHER HOLY HABITS

Fellowship deepens and grows around the sharing of food and stories.

MAKING MORE DISCIPLES

FELLOWSHIP

Providing meals for the lonely, housebound, homeless or families on low incomes is an outworking of **Sharing Resources**, **Serving** and **Generosity**. The meals can be a source of **Gladness** to those who partake, and of course food offered in the context of a party or celebration also gladdens the heart.

SHARING RESOURCES

GLADNESS AND GENEROSITY

SERVING

GOING FURTHER WITH THE HABIT

DEVELOPING FURTHER PRACTICES OF EATING TOGETHER

Interfaith meal ☺

Invite friends from other faith traditions over for an evening of food and interscriptural dialogue (the story of Noah is a brilliant one to start with). The intention here is not to convert, but rather to be engaged and present to other faith stories and to get to know those neighbours better.

Community meal

Invite your neighbours or acquaintances for a meal in your home to share community with them.

As a church, partner with a charity or local organisation and share in their work of enabling others to **Eat Together** – for example those working with homeless people, refugees, asylum seekers, those with mental health issues, young people, older people, victims of domestic abuse.

Tackling food waste and food poverty

Many projects manage to combine both aid to the community and a strong sense of redressing the huge problem of wasted food. Some organisations working in this area are:

- The Trussell Trust (**www.trusselltrust.org**) – national network of food banks.
- Food Cycle (**www.foodcycle.org.uk**) – intercepting and distributing food that would otherwise be wasted.
- FareShare (**www.fareshare.org.uk**) – intercepting and distributing surplus food to community organisations.
- The Real Junk Food Project (**www.therealjunkfoodproject.org**) – a network of pay-as-you-feel cafés using intercepted food.

Eating and talking together

Eating Together is an integral part of many discipleship and evangelism resources and communities, most notably Alpha and Messy Church.

A number of resources have also been developed explicitly to share and explore faith within the context of **Eating Together**. Table Talk is one of these (**www.table-talk.org**). This is a conversational game that creates an opportunity to explore some of life's biggest questions. A range of 'games' are available including Table Talk for Christmas, for Easter, for friends, for women, for men and for a wide range of specific age groups.

Alternatively, next time you have a 'faith supper' or 'bring and share tea', ask everyone to find out something about one ingredient in the dish they bring. This might be as simple as the country of origin, it might be something about how it is produced or processed, or it might be a surprise ingredient or one of those hidden 'additives'. There are lots of ways to use the information:

- discussions around the table
- a quiz
- guessing games (which dish contains x, where does x come from, how far has x travelled)
- food miles
- time taken to grow
- world cuisines – how much rice is eaten in China every day.

When the habit of **Eating Together** is established, you might become more specific about the piece of information to find out so that the quiz or discussion can be more focused.

You can lead into thinking about:

- how our simple meal here is connected to other parts of the world
- access to choice and variety
- distribution of wealth
- food links to education
- cultural restrictions around food.

Deeper information and stories can be found by looking at Fairtrade websites. From these, other resources such as posters and DVDs might be introduced if the occasion allows.

A variation is to ask everyone to bring something which includes a fairly traded or locally sourced ingredient and then to try to guess which ingredient it is.

New Monasticism

New Monasticism is reconnecting many with ancient practices or habits of Christian discipleship including **Eating Together**, a habit that was at the heart of the life Jesus shared with his first disciples. Conventional wisdom has it that Jesus chose twelve disciples in order to represent the twelve tribes of Israel. An alternative school of thought suggests that Jesus chose twelve because this was the number that could typically be seated around a meal table at the time.

The first Christian communities (churches) met in homes too and gathered around the table. The practice of meeting in homes allowed the early Christians to continue the patterns of table **Fellowship** found in the Gospels. As biblical commentator Bradley Blue points out:

> The early believers met in houses not by default alone… but deliberately because the house setting provided the facilities which were of paramount importance for the gathering. For example, the culinary appurtenances necessary for the meal.
>
> Bradley Blue, 'Acts and the House Church' in David W.J. Gill and Conrad Gempf (eds), *The Book of Acts in its First Century Setting*, Vol 2 (William B. Eerdmans, 1994), p. 121

Many contemporary New Monastic communities gather around a meal table to eat, talk, pray and break bread together. In *A New Monastic Handbook*, Mark Berry describes how the safespace community in Telford, born of a partnership between the Anglican Diocese of Lichfield and the Church Mission Society, was formed around a meal table:

> We make and eat a meal, we invite guests to join us, we spend time in reflection and meditation on Scripture, we write, create and use liturgy, we break bread together and we gently and generously hold each other accountable. We have been surprised how vital it has been to eat together as family, with no 'Head of the table', as equals and how real the breaking of bread feels in this context. We have welcomed guests from all over the world and from other faiths to share and reflect with us on God, Spirituality, Mission and Community.
>
> Ian Mobsby and Mark Berry, *A New Monastic Handbook* (Canterbury Press, 2014), p. 178

Notice how in the last sentence Mark speaks of welcoming guests. A key feature of New Monasticism is how it fuses a depth of **Fellowship** with a missional heart of hospitality. As Ian Adams points out:

'The abbot's table,' says St Benedict, 'must always be with guests and travellers.'

Ian Adams, *Cave, Refectory, Road* (Canterbury Press, 2010), p. 24

This, of course, goes straight to the heart of Jesus' instructions in Luke 14:12–14:

> When you give a luncheon or a dinner, do not invite your friends or your brothers or your relatives or rich neighbours, in case they may invite you in return, and you would be repaid. But when you give a banquet, invite the poor, the crippled, the lame, and the blind. And you will be blessed, because they cannot repay you, for you will be repaid at the resurrection of the righteous.

A stunning example of a Christian community committed to this way of living is the Community of Sant Egidio. Have a look at how they do Christmas lunch: **www. santegidio.org/pageID/35/langID/en/The-Christmas-Lunch.html**.

You might like to reflect upon this experience in the light of your tradition or denomination. How might it be possible for you to use **Eating Together** as a way of deepening **Fellowship** and resourcing mission? Are you being called to form a new Christian community – a fresh expression of church – and might gathering around a table and **Eating Together** be a way to begin forming that new community?

Around the world in food

Training or tuition could be given in cooking different national dishes or regional cuisine. Churches or individuals within congregations could offer to teach others their speciality dish – whether this is a Chinese church sharing some authentic Chinese recipes, a Zimbabwean fellowship cooking a national dish or an individual with a particular speciality. You could also involve local people who work in the food industry, or have experience in international cuisine, to come and share with your congregation or small group.

Feasting and fasting

(Adapted from Andrew Roberts, *Holy Habits*, Malcolm Down Publishing, 2016, pp. 194–95.)

For deepening discipleship, many testify to the value of living rhythmically. The Holy Habit of **Eating Together** lends itself to a rhythm of life that is both formative of discipleship and missional. Gathering with fellow disciples to celebrate major festivals with the sharing of food has ancient pedigree, going deep into our Judaeo-Christian history. Christmas, Easter, Pentecost and Harvest provide quarterly opportunities for **Eating Together** with **Gladness** and for inviting others to come and taste and see that the Lord is good.

Alongside the habits of feasting and **Eating Together** is the ancient faith practice of fasting: abstaining from food for a shorter or longer period of time as a sign of devotion and character-building discipline, in order to create space to pray and explore the Bible. It is a habit that Jesus himself practised.

Fasting reminds us that we are sustained 'by every word that comes from the mouth of God' (Matthew 4:4). While fasting, we are not so much abstaining from food as we are feasting on the word of God. Fasting is feasting!

Fasting develops personal holiness. It also contributes to the social holiness of justice. When we fast, we identify with those for whom being hungry is not a choice; we stand against the might of the marketers and those who espouse the lie that greed is good. And we can, if we choose, cheerfully share the resources saved with those who have less.

As well as personal fasting, some Christians have practised having very simple, inexpensive meals once a week to identify with the many people around the world who eat simply or not at all – not out of choice, but from simple lack of food or other necessity. The money saved by having such 'hunger lunches' is then given to support those in need elsewhere.

As with feasting, fasting can fit well with a rhythm of life. Many disciples of Jesus practise a weekly day of fasting. Many others consciously practise the habit during Lent. At this time and others, fasting does not have to be limited to abstaining from food. We can fast from other things too: from shopping or social media to being critical or cynical. Fasting in ways like these can also help to develop personal discipline and holiness. They can also be ways by which we release resources to bless others.

If fasting from food is a habit you have not tried and would like to consider, do make sure that it is safe to do so medically. Have a word with your doctor. You never know – they might be intrigued as to why you want to do it!

Sharing your story

Jesus loved to eat with people but he was criticised for practising this Holy Habit: 'The Son of Man, on the other hand, feasts and drinks, and you say, "He's a glutton and a drunkard, and a friend of tax collectors and other sinners!"' (Luke 7:34, NLT).

As you are formed and transformed by practising the Holy Habit of **Eating Together**, how will you share the stories of Jesus **Eating Together** with all sorts of different people?

How will you share your part in that story as you eat with others?

What stories will others tell about you, as an individual and in the community in which you work out your discipleship, about how **Eating Together** has formed and transformed you?

ARTS AND MEDIA

There are many films and books containing scenes about **Eating Together** which could be used as an illustration in worship. However, it is suggested that the following films and books are watched or read in their entirety and followed by a discussion to go deeper into the topic of **Eating Together**.

The meal table can be a particularly good place to explore deep or sensitive matters which can be raised by many of these arts and media resources.

Films

ᛘᛘᛘ Arthur Christmas (U, 2011, 1h37m)

Grandsanta, Santa Claus, Mrs Claus, Steve and Arthur all sit down for a meal after their busy night delivering gifts. Unfortunately, they have let their work get to them and none of them are too keen to share food with each other. Except for Arthur, who recognises how it is more than just food, but family sharing in a relationship.

- What's the most important part of any meal?
- Does this film remind you of any of the meals Jesus shared with people?

Babette's Feast (U, 1987, 1h42m)

A French chef takes refuge from the Revolution on a remote island among people of a strict Protestant sect.

- What does Babette help them to see about who the centre of their community really is?
- 'This is a night of grace…' – how does eating a feast together change people's relationships?

Chocolat (12, 2000, 2h1m)

A young woman and her daughter, who seem oblivious to the rules but alive to charity, challenge the people of a small French town, who are complacent in their Lenten observance. Based on a book of the same name.

- How does the film challenge our practice of welcome and hospitality?
- How can food be a barrier to proclaiming the gospel?
- How can we practise the habits of **Gladness and Generosity** as we develop the habit of **Eating Together**?

- How can we cultivate the principles of **Eating Together** while respecting Lenten observance or other religious fasting and while taking into consideration special dietary needs including diabetes, food allergies or intolerances, eating disorders or other restrictions around food and drink?

Group study book available: *Christ and the Chocolaterie* by Hilary Brand (DLT, 2002).

👪 Cloudy with a Chance of Meatballs (U, 2009, 1h30m)

This film talks about why we should appreciate the food we have. The town's greed for bigger and better food, combined with Flint's desire to impress, leads to disaster: the entire world is almost destroyed by greed.

- What does this film say about our desire for food?
- Are there ways we can eat with those in need in our communities?

👪 Ratatouille (U, 2007, 1h51m)

A film which explores the habit of **Eating Together** in sometimes unconventional ways!

As the critic sits down for his meal and tastes the most basic and simple of food, he is transported back to a time of family. The modest food he is given helps him to remember where it all began: with his mother's love. Not only can food be a real example of love, but sometimes the most modest food can be the most meaningful if we bring our relationships and love with it.

- What's the best meal in the film? Why?
- What ingredients make a good meal (if we're trying to practise the habit of **Eating Together**)?
- At the end of the film, as the critic sits down for his meal, he is transported back to a family meal. How does this speak of the place of relationships and love in **Eating Together**?

Books: fiction

Are there people in your church or local community who would like to discuss some of these books at a book club? Guidance on how to form these is widely available online, and you could also ask denominational training officers for help.

👪 Charlie and the Chocolate Factory
Roald Dahl (Puffin Books, 1964)

The desire for chocolate and sweets is integral to the story of this book. Two film versions of this book have been made, in very different styles.

- How does **Eating Together** in Charlie's family differ from the experience and expectations of the other children in the story?

- Does your experience of **Eating Together** differ from the experience and expectations of others?

👪 Daisy: Eat Your Peas
Kes Gray, Nick Sharratt (Red Fox Picture Books, 2009)

This book helps children deal with more difficult issues of **Eating Together**.

- What food do you find difficult to eat up?
- Why do you think our parents make us 'eat up'?

👪 The Friday Nights of Nana
Amy Hest, Claire A. Nivola (Walker Books, 2002)

A Jewish story about preparing for the Sabbath and the meal that the family will share together. This book may be out of print, but is often available second hand.

- How does your family share special meals together?
- Why is it important to eat together?

👪 Hillytown Biscuit Church
Ruth Whiter (Christian Education, 2008)

This book gives insight into what children and young people think about going to church.

- Does your church have refreshments after the service?

- What does this book tell you about the importance of biscuits?

👪 Mama Panya's Pancakes: A village tale from Kenya
Mary Chamberlain (Barefoot Books, 2006)

A book about pooling resources and sharing to make a meal.

- How about having a pancake party and inviting your friends?

Purple Hibiscus
Chimamanda Ngozi Adichie (Fourth Estate, 2013)

- Look at the relaxed and formal styles of **Eating Together** in the different settings in this book. Who eats with whom and what does this say about their relationship?

The Settler's Cookbook: A memoir of love, migration and food
Yasmin Alibhai-Brown (new edition, Portobello Books, 2010)

Through the personal story of Yasmin's family and the food and recipes they've shared together, *The Settler's Cookbook* tells the history of Indian migration to the UK via East Africa. Her family was part of the mass exodus from India to East Africa during the height of British imperial expansion, fleeing famine and lured by the prospect of prosperity under the empire.

- Are there people in your congregation or local community who could share their experiences of migration and food?

Books: non-fiction

Cave, Refectory, Road
Ian Adams (Canterbury Press, 2010)

A new monastic perspective on the practice of **Eating Together**.

- How could your church be a cave, a place of retreat and renewal; a refectory, a place of hospitality; or a road, a place of journeying out to share food, faith and life?

Extending the Table: Recipes and stories from Afghanistan to Zambia in the spirit of more-with-less
Joetta Handrich Schlabach and Kristina Mast Burnett (eds) (revised edition, Herald Press, 2014)

The recipes in this fascinating book provide opportunities for people to taste food from around the world, and the book also offers insight into how hospitality is practised in different cultures.

- How could the recipes and stories in this book help you to explore **Eating Together** with your family, friends and neighbours?

Friends, Faith and Feasts
Sylvia Hart (Inspire Publishing, 2006)

A cookery book based around Christian festivals and feast days.

- Could you have a church meal where people bring different dishes to share? Why not invite groups in the community for a free meal?

From Tablet to Table
Leonard Sweet (NavPress, 2014)

A very helpful exploration of the biblical tradition of table fellowship and how it can be effective today in forming discipleship communities.

- How can **Eating Together** truly be a sacred encounter? How can it be spiritually and physically nourishing?

A Meal with Jesus: Discovering grace, community and mission around the table
Tim Chester (Inter-Varsity Press, 2011)

Remembering meals that Jesus shared, this book explores the theology of **Eating Together** and invites the reader to consider hospitality not only as **Fellowship** and **Serving**, but as a means of grace.

- Could the ideas in this book be explored with your church leadership team, event organisers or catering team as they reconsider what it means to **Eat Together**?

Sacred Food: Cooking for spiritual nourishment
Elisabeth Luard (New Print, 2004)

Celebrating the power of food to nourish souls and its vital part in religious ceremonies and secular celebrations, this cookbook offers insights into food that go far beyond recipes.

- Could each group in the church be invited to share 'Sacred Food' together?

Articles and online media

The Work of the People

The Work of the People (**www.theworkofthepeople.com**) is an online community founded by Travis Reed. It features short videos on a variety of topics.

- The Table (**www.theworkofthepeople.com/the-table**, 3m17s)
- Back to the Table (**www.theworkofthepeople.com/back-to-the-table**, 3m4s)
- Comforted at the Table (**www.theworkofthepeople.com/comforted-at-the-table**, 4m7s)
- Table Benediction (**www.theworkofthepeople.com/table-benediction**, 1m53s)

Spoken word

The Table (**youtu.be/-vgv7bMwD9k**, or search YouTube for 'The Table Spoken Word', 2m51s)

Eat, Act, Pray

The Christian Aid Collective's campaign to spark conversation and discussion, making mealtimes about more than food (**www.christianaidcollective.org/eat-act-pray-teaser** or search the Christian Aid Collective site for 'Eat, Act, Pray', 1m37s)

The Joy of Food

A *National Geographic* article with some great images and quotes (**www.nationalgeographic.com/foodfeatures/joy-of-food**).

Food stories

First-hand audio accounts of the changes in eating habits and rituals and traditions since the 1930s from the British Library, which also illustrate social change in the UK (**www.bl.uk/learning/citizenship/foodstories**).

Eating Together

A number of articles exploring the benefits of **Eating Together**:

- BBC: Should families eat together every night? (**www.bbc.co.uk/food/0/26068619**)
- *Daily Mail*: Families who eat together stay together (**www.dailymail.co.uk/debate/article-1313916/Families-eat-stay-together.html**)
- Spark People: The benefits of **Eating Together** (**www.sparkpeople.com/resource/nutrition_articles.asp?id=439**)
- Eartheasy: Why eating family meals together is still important today (**www.eartheasy.com/blog/2011/12/why-eating-family-meals-together-is-still-important-today**)

Good News Stories

House of Bread (**youtu.be/ojw2cHXQpbU** or search YouTube for 'Good News Stories with Nick'). This story is also listed in **Breaking Bread**.

Music

The following songs may help you to explore and reflect further on this habit.

Harvest for the World
The Isley Brothers/The Christians

A powerful song that mixes thanksgiving with a cry on behalf of those in need.

👪 Fast Food Song
Fast Food Rockers

This and the next song are two fun songs to start conversation about the importance of **Eating Together** with primary-aged children.

👪 Lunchtime Song
Nick Jr

Poetry

A number of poems are referenced below. Choose one to reflect on.

You may wish to consider some of the following questions:

- What does this poem say to you about **Eating Together**?
- Which images do you find helpful or unhelpful?
- How is your practice of **Eating Together** challenged by this poem?
- Could you write a poem to share with others the virtues of **Eating Together**?

Chocolate Cake
Michael Rosen

Why not make a chocolate cake and eat it together while discussing the poem?

We are One
Ian Adams, from *Unfurling* (Canterbury Press, 2015)

Psalm 133 Redux
Carla Grosch-Miller, from *Psalms Redux* (Canterbury Press, 2014)

Food For Risen Bodies – II
Michael Symmons Roberts, from *Corpus* (Jonathan Cape, 2004)

The Five Thousand

Eularia Clarke (1914–70): oil, 1962, 65 x 62 cm.
From the Methodist Modern Art Collection, © TMCP, used with permission.
You can download this image from: www.methodist.org.uk/artcollection

This painting is based on the account of the feeding of the 5,000 recorded in all four Gospels. Eularia Clarke, a teacher of art in schools, follows Matthew's account in which women and children are present but her work reminds us more of a 20th-century church picnic than the biblical miracle.

- Although the focus is on **Eating Together**, there is also a sense of listening and learning. Which elements of the painting suggest this most?
- If you had to select a detail of the painting in order to illustrate 'grace', which part would it be?
- Draw or paint an occasion when you have shared a memorable meal. In what ways might you describe it as sacred?

Hospitality

This photo shows **Eating Together**, hospitality and sharing in a particular situation. What does it say to you? In what ways is it challenging or reaffirming?

In a society in which research tells us that fewer and fewer families eat together, explore where, when, why and how **Eating Together** is important to you.

Credits

In addition to the Holy Habits editorial/development team, contributions to this booklet also came from: Vicki Atkinson, Fiona Barker, Andrew Brazier, Tina Brooker, Andy Clark, Rachel Frank, Jean Hamilton, Peter Harding, Ken Howcroft, Neil Johnson, Tony Malcolm, Andrew Mason, Sarah Middleton, Tom Milton, Martyn Payne, Helen Pollard, Kathryn Price, Michele Simms and University of Birmingham chaplaincy students.

'This set of ten resources will enable churches and individuals to begin to establish "habits of faithfulness". In the United Reformed Church, we are calling this process of developing discipleship, "Walking the Way: Living the life of Jesus today" and I have no doubt that this comprehensive set of resources will enable us to do just that.'
Revd Richard Church, Deputy General Secretary (Discipleship), United Reformed Church

'Here are some varied and rich resources to help further deepen our discipleship of Christ, encouraging and enabling us to adopt the life-transforming habits that make for following Jesus.'
Revd Dr Martyn Atkins, Team Leader & Superintendent Minister, Methodist Central Hall, Westminster

'The Holy Habits resources will help you, your church, your fellowship group, to engage in a journey of discovery about what it really means to be a disciple today. I know you will be encouraged, challenged and inspired as you read and work your way through each chapter. There is lots to study together and pray about, and that can only be good as our churches today seek to bring about the kingdom of God.'
Revd Loraine Mellor, President of the Methodist Conference 2017/18

'The Holy Habits resources help weave the spiritual through everyday life. They're a great tool that just get better with use. They help us grow in our desire to follow Jesus as their concern is formation not simply information.'
Olive Fleming Drane and John Drane

'The Holy Habits resources are an insightful and comprehensive manual for living in the way of Jesus in the 21st century: an imaginative, faithful and practical gift for the church that will sustain and invigorate our life and mission in a demanding world. The Holy Habits resources are potentially transformational for a church.'
Revd Ian Adams, Mission Spirituality Adviser for Church Mission Society

'To understand the disciplines of the Christian life without practising them habitually is like owning a fine collection of soap but never having a wash. The team behind Holy Habits knows this, which is why they have produced these excellent and practical resources. Use them, and by God's grace you will grow in holiness.'
Paul Bayes, Bishop of Liverpool

'The Holy Habits resources are a rich mine of activities for all ages to help change minds, attitudes and behaviours. I love the way many different people groups are represented and celebrated, and the constant references to the complex realities of 21st-century life.'
Lucy Moore, Founder of BRF's Messy Church